the MOTHER of a MOVEMENT

JEANNE MANFORD

ALLY, ACTIVIST, and CO-FOUNDER of PFLAG

written by
ROB SANDERS

illustrated by
SAM KALDA

What does a mom do?

Some listen and love.

Learn and lead.

Some want the best for their children and to make life better for them, too.

That's what some moms do.

What did this mom do?
She raised three children.
Caring. Nurturing. Teaching.
And she taught children in elementary school.
Caring. Nurturing. Teaching.

That's what
Jeanne Manford did.

What does a teacher-mom do?
Some bandage knees and wipe away tears.
Settle arguments and teach manners.
Some know each child is special—unique.
Show children that they can be who they dream to be.

That's **what Jeanne did.**

Year after year, her students grew up.

So did her own children.

What does the mom of grown children do?

Some listen and love.

Learn and lead.

Some watch their children discover themselves.

That's what **Jeanne** did.

Then one day, Jeanne's son Morty told her,
"I'm gay."

What does the mom of a gay son do?

Some turn their children away. Some turn their backs.

Some shed tears. Some share fears.

But others hold their children close.

Hug them tight.

And listen, love, and learn.

That's what Jeanne did.

Morty was her son.

He was gay.

She loved him.

That was that.

Others weren't so accepting.

Once when Morty protested the unfair treatment of the LGBTQ+ community, he was attacked.

Beaten.

He ended up in the hospital.

What does a mom do when her son is mistreated?

She could comfort him. She could confront her own feelings.

She could take action. She could write a letter.

She could tell the truth. Her truth.

That's what Jeanne did.

Her letter was printed in the *New York Post*.

In 1972, most mothers did not tell people their children were gay.

Never had a mother written to a newspaper about her gay child.

Jeanne did.

I have...

a gay...

son...

Soon Morty began to receive phone calls.

Many couldn't believe his mother had written such a letter.

Perhaps they wished their own mothers had done the same.

... and I love him.

When everyone knows her son is gay, what does a mom do?

She could listen. She could love.

She could learn and lead.

She could speak up.

She could show support.

That's what
Jeanne did.

Morty asked Jeanne to march with him in the Christopher Street Parade.

Jeanne made time. And she made a sign.

She showed up. She stood up—side-by-side with her son.

People in the crowd cheered for the mom with the sign.

PARENTS of Gays: UNITE in SUPPORT for our CHILDREN

GAY LIBERAT

Soon, Jeanne began to receive phone calls and letters.

People stopped her on the street.

Some had been kicked out of their homes and abandoned by their families.

Some were parents and family members who wanted to do better for their LGBTQ+ children.

What does a mom do when other children are mistreated?

What does a mom do when other parents need help?

She could listen. She could love.

She could learn and lead.

She could make new friends.

The friends might become allies.

The allies might become a force.

That's what
Jeanne did.

She organized meetings.
She brought parents together.
She founded a new organization.

PFLA

FATHER
OF A
-AY

PROUD
of my
GAY BROTHER

PARENTS
IN LOVING
OF OUR

TS

It became known as PFLAG, an organization for parents, families, and allies of LGBTQ+ people.

OF GAYS

SUPPOR

CHILDR

I WILL NOT BE A CLOSET MOTHER

And she kept being a mom.

Caring. Nurturing. Teaching.

A mom to her own children.

A mom to others who needed her.

A mom to mothers, fathers, grandparents, aunts, uncles, and all those with children from the LGBTQ+ community—all those who wanted to listen and love and learn and lead.

That's what Jeanne Manford did.

She started a movement.

UNITED IN LOVE — WE ARE FAMILY

PFLAG

And the movement spread.

From parent to parent.

Family to family.

City to city.

Today PFLAG works to grow
proud people,

loving families,

safe communities,

and a diverse and inclusive world.

It all began with one mother.

It all began with Jeanne Manford.

She listened. She loved.

She learned. She led.

Caring. Nurturing. Teaching.

That's what this mom did.

Discussion Guide

When reading any book of nonfiction, questions may arise. As a book is read again and again, children's questions often go deeper and deeper. Create an atmosphere where children feel their questions are welcome by being honest, succinct, and by providing answers based in fact. Feel free to ask a child, "What do you think?" or "What are you feeling?" Remember, you don't have to have an answer to every question. There's nothing wrong with saying, "I don't know" or "Let me think about that" or "Let me try to find an answer." The following are some sample responses to questions that children may have after reading or listening to this book.

Why was it that in 1972 most mothers did not tell people that their children were LGBTQ+? Is that still the case today?

In 1972, people were led to believe that being a member of the LGBTQ+ community was bad or wrong. Some even believed being queer meant a person was ill. Slowly, over time, with more and more information, views began to change. As more members of the LGBTQ+ community came out and told their stories, more parents, families, and friends began to change their thinking and became more accepting and affirming.

While many things are better for members of the LGBTQ+ community today, sadly there are still people who are not accepting and who discriminate against members of the community. There are still some parents who do not accept their children. Members of the LGBTQ+ community still can lose their jobs under state law, and can still lose their homes and their families simply because of who they are. But many others find love and acceptance within their families and friends. Others create "chosen families," encircling themselves with those who are accepting, loving, and affirming.

What is discrimination and why does it happen?

Discrimination is the unfair treatment of people or groups of people based on who they are. People are discriminated against because of race, gender identity or expression, age, sexual orientation, and other characteristics. Discrimination often is caused by fear, misunderstanding, anger, and/or hate.

What did it mean for Jeanne to show up and march with Morty?

Morty invited his mother to march with him, and must have been pleased, happy, and proud that she walked side-by-side with him in the Christopher Street Liberation Day March in 1972. We know that others in the crowd were surprised that a mom would be marching with her gay son. Their surprise was mixed with happiness and hope—hope that other parents might be accepting of their LGBTQ+ children, too. But there were other things that Jeanne's marching meant. It meant that at least one parent was not ashamed of her LGBTQ+ child. It meant that views about accepting those within the LGBTQ+ community were beginning to change. And it meant that other parents had an example of how they could support their children who might identify as lesbian, gay, bisexual, transgender, queer, or questioning.

Why would it have been important for parents, families, and friends of LGBTQ+ people to be able to meet together?

Sometimes being with someone who is experiencing the same things you are provides comfort and support. That's how many have felt when attending PFLAG meetings. There, in a safe place, people can find support, encouragement, and help from others. They can also see that others started their journeys in one place and moved from fear or worry to affirmation, understanding, and love.

What does PFLAG do?

PFLAG has three pillars of work: Support, Education, and Advocacy. PFLAG provides support for parents, family members, allies to the LGBTQ+ community, and LGBTQ+ people themselves through meetings led by local PFLAG chapters, and PFLAG National, PFLAG's national organization. PFLAG provides education to people who are still learning about LGBTQ+ people and the issues important to them. PFLAG also engages in advocacy, speaking out against practices that are harmful and discriminatory to members of the LGBTQ+ community, working for the fair and safe education of LGBTQ+ students, working to ensure equality for LGBTQ+ people through local, state, and federal legislation, and more.

What is an ally and how can I be one?**

In the LGBTQ+ community, an ally is someone who is supportive of LGBTQ+ people, behaves in supportive ways, and invites others to be allies, too. While Jeanne Manford is a famous ally, throughout history there are people just like you who have been willing to provide support, encouragement, and help. Here are some simple ways YOU can be an ally:

START BY LEARNING.
Allies are always learning so they can do more and help educate others. You won't always have all the answers, and that's okay! If you make a mistake, apologize and learn how to do better next time.

DON'T LET FEAR STOP YOU.
There are lots of reasons why people might be afraid to be allies. Maybe they're nervous about speaking up. Maybe they aren't sure where to start. Listen to what others tell you. Figure out what feels scary to you. Then you can figure out how to take action.

BE ACTIVE.
Start with something simple, like putting a rainbow sticker on your backpack and telling friends why it's there. Use what you learn from books like this one to talk about why you care and help others be allies. Most of all? Treat others with kindness and respect.

THERE ARE MANY WAYS TO BE AN ALLY.
There's no one way to be an ally. Some of us are loud and visible. Others help in quieter ways. But we're all working to reach the same goals of equality and respect for everyone.

**The information in this section is adapted from *Guide to Being a Straight Ally* and *Guide to Being a Trans Ally* by PFLAG National, part of the Straight for Equality™ program ©2022 PFLAG, Inc.

To Think About and Discuss

Use the open-ended questions below to begin conversations with the children in your family, class, club, or organization.

- **When was a time you were an ally to someone? Why did you do it? How did it feel to stand up for someone else?**

- **Has there been a time when someone was an ally to you?**

- **Do you think it's important to be an ally to others? Why or why not?**

Glossary

activist—someone who speaks out and protests about a cause or issue, especially a political or social cause.

ally—a person or group who works with others for a common cause or purpose, especially a supporter of a marginalized group, who is usually not a member of the group.

co-founder—someone who begins or forms something with another.

founded—to set up or begin something that will last.

gay—used to describe a person who loves and is attracted to a person of the same gender, often used to describe men in the LGBTQ+ community but can be used for women too.

lesbian—a woman who loves and is attracted to other women.

LGBTQ+—Lesbian, gay, bisexual, transgender, queer or questioning. The + represents all the other identities of those in the community. When the events of this story occurred, the community was often referred to only as the *gay community* or the *gay and lesbian community*. However, those terms left out many vital members of the larger community.

nurturing—providing protection, comfort, and support; providing for the needs of another.

protest—an act to show objection, disapproval, or dissent. Protests are often about things a person or group have no power over but want to see changed.

Meet Morty Manford— LGBTQ+ Activist and Pioneer

The second of Jeanne and Jules Manford's three children, Morty Manford, was born on September 17, 1950. Morty is one of many whose contributions to the struggle for LGBTQ+ rights have nearly been forgotten. As a 19-year-old, Morty was at the Stonewall Inn on June 28, 1969, when an uprising occurred that changed the LGBTQ+ community forever. The event was a turning point for Morty, too. Ten days later he was in Philadelphia taking part in a demonstration at Independence Hall. The flame of activism had been lit in Morty.

In 1972, while protesting at the 50th annual Inner Circle dinner, Morty and other protestors were attacked and beaten. Morty's injuries landed him in the hospital. He later testified at the trial of his attacker. Though the man was acquitted, outrage over the attack eventually led to New York City's first gay-rights law.

When attending college at Columbia University, Morty helped organize one of the first gay groups on a college campus, Gay People at Columbia. He is credited with coining the term "zaps" to describe the protests and pressure put on politicians to urge them to support gay rights. Morty helped establish many organizations including the Gay Activists Alliance and the Lambda Club. He headed several gay rights organizations including serving as director of the Lambda Legal Defense and Education Fund. Morty wrote and spoke frequently about the gay rights movement.

After graduating from law school, Morty worked for many years as a staff attorney and supervising attorney at the Legal Aid Society of New York working with clients who could not afford an attorney. He became an Assistant Attorney General of the State of New York in 1987.

On May 14, 1992, Morty died of AIDS-related complications. He was 42 years old. His speaking, writing, organizing, and participation in everything from demonstrations to marches, pickets to sit-ins, zaps to protests contributed to the hard-earned rights the LGBTQ+ community now has. Undoubtedly, Morty would agree that there is more work to do.

The History of PFLAG

The idea for PFLAG began in 1972 when Jeanne Manford joined her son, Morty, in New York City's Christopher Street Liberation Day March. During the march, many LGBTQ+ community members came to Jeanne and asked her to speak with their parents. The idea for a support group formed in Jeanne's mind. Morty supported his mom's idea. Jeanne's husband, Jules, immediately joined in the effort, making the endeavor a true family affair. Morty, Jeanne, and Jules, along with other LGBTQ+ people and their parents, founded the original organization. The first meeting took place on March 11, 1973, at the Metropolitan-Duane Methodist Church in Greenwich Village (now the Church of the Village). Around 20 people attended.

Suzanne Manford Swan, Jeanne's daughter and Morty's sister, reports that students often said of her mother, "If Mrs. Manford says it's ok to be homosexual, then I'm ok." That sentiment was pervasive in the new organization, too.

Word about the organization spread from community to community, town to town, state to state, and similar groups were formed around the country. The meetings became a place for parents of LGBTQ+ people to gather, to find support and encouragement, and to have a safe place to talk about their concerns. As the LGBTQ+ community grew and expanded and became more inclusive, so did those who attended meetings. In 1979, after the National March for Gay and Lesbian Rights in Washington, D.C., representatives from these various groups met together for the first time. In 1991, they formed PFLAG National, a national organization in the United States.

The organization has had many names over the years. The original name of the organization was POG, or Parents of Gays. Over the years, the change in the social landscape ushered in modifications to that name, moving from POG to Parents FLAG, to Parents, Families, and Friends of Lesbians and Gays. In 2014, to reflect the wide range of PFLAG members, those it serves, and the inclusive work the organization does, the organization became known simply as PFLAG.

PFLAG is the first and largest organization for LGBTQ+ people, their parents and families, and allies. The organization has nearly 400 chapters and 250,000 members and supporters. These members and supporters are people from various age groups, from all walks of life, and live in cities, towns, suburbs, and rural areas. PFLAG organizations now exist all around the world, from China to Australia to all across Europe and Korea.

SOURCE: PFLAG.org

The Christopher Street March

Jeanne Manford and Morty (on Jeanne's right, your left) march
in the 1972 Christopher Street Liberation Day March.

When Jeanne Manford marched with her son, Morty, in the 1972 Christopher Street Liberation Day March, she was participating in the third march of its kind. The first Christopher Street Liberation Day March was held on June 28, 1970, to commemorate the uprising at the Stonewall Inn that occurred a year before. That march inspired the Pride marches, festivals, and events that are now held around the world each June to celebrate the events at the Stonewall Inn and the LGBTQ+ community, its members and their accomplishments, and to raise awareness of issues facing the community.

The homemade poster Jeanne carried in the 1972 Christopher Street Liberation Day March read: "PARENTS of Gays: UNITE in SUPPORT for our CHILDREN."
Credit: Manuscripts and Archives Division, The New York Public Library

A Medal for Jeanne

On February 15, 2013, a month after Jeanne's Manford's death, President Barack Obama posthumously awarded her the Presidential Citizens Medal, the nation's second highest civilian honor. The medal was presented to Jeanne's only surviving child, Suzanne Manford Swan.

During the presentation ceremony, President Obama said: "When Jeanne Manford learned that her son Morty had been badly beaten up at a gay rights demonstration, nobody would have faulted her for bringing him home, holding him close, just focusing on her child . . . But instead, she wrote to the local newspaper and took to the streets with a simple message: No matter who her son was—no matter who he loved— she loved him, and wouldn't put up with this kind of nonsense. And in that simple act, she inspired a movement and gave rise to a national organization that has given so much support to parents and families and friends, and helped to change this country."

Suzanne Manford Swan, daughter of Jeanne Manford, received the Presidential Citizens Medal on behalf of her mother from President Barack Obama.

Quote source:

President Barack Obama (2013). *Remarks by the president at presentation of 2012 Presidential Citizens Medals.* https://obamawhitehouse.archives.gov/the-press-office/2013/02/15/remarks-president-presentation-2012-presidential-citizens-medals

A Selected List of Sources

NEWSPAPER ARTICLES

Frank Jackman (1971, October 21). McG Offers Economic Plan. *Daily News*.

William Proctor (1972, June 27). Three testify Maye beat gay protestors. *Daily News*.

William Proctor (1982, July 6). Fireman Maye acquitted in Hilton hassle. *Daily News*.

Ann Ledesma (1974, April 19). Gay president's son to tell story at Rutgers. *The Central New Jersey Home News*.

Daily News (1974, May 12). A serious look at gay rights.

Marilyn Goldstein (1979, August 19). Our child is gay. *Newsday* (Nassau Edition).

Anna Quindlen (1992, May 30). Love that does dare speak its name. *The Vancouver Sun*.

Holly Favino (1993, May 30). Always proud of her family. *Newsday*.

PAPERS/COLLECTION/ARCHIVES

Jeanne Manford papers. Manuscripts and Archives Division, The New York Public Library. Call no. MssCol 1857. http://archives.nypl.org/mss/1857

Morty Manford papers. Manuscripts and Archives Division, The New York Public Library. Call no. MssCol 1858. https://archives.nypl.org/mss/1858

PODCASTS

Making Gay History—The Podcast. (2016, November). Jeanne & Morty Manford (No. 6). https://makinggayhistory.com/podcast/episode-1-6/

Making Gay History—The Podcast. (2017, December). Morty Manford (No. 102). https://makinggayhistory.com/podcast/morty-manford/

Making Gay History—The Podcast. (2019, January). Stonewall 50 minisode: Morty Mandford. https://makinggayhistory.com/podcast/stonewall-50-minisode-2-morty-manford/

PFLAG

About PFLAG https://pflag.org/about

PFLAG San Francisco (2013, February 2). *Jeanne Manford, PFLAG's founder, speaks to PFLAG San Francisco* [Video]. YouTube. https:/youtube.com/watch?v=Aq5OcqbjpNE

VIDEOS

Rachel Maddow (2013, January 11). *Jeanne Manford, model for parental love*. MSNBC. https://msnbc.com/rachel-maddow-show/watch/jeanne-manford-model-for-parental-love-14467139531

To Learn More About the LGBTQ+ Community

Gayle E. Pitman (2021). *Evelyn hooker and the fairy project*. Magination Press.

Gayle E. Pitman (2018). *Sewing the rainbow: A story about Gilbert Baker*. Magination Press.

Gayle E. Pitman (2014). *This day in June*. Magination Press.

Gayle E. Pitman (2017). *When you look out the window: How Phyllis Lyon and Del Martin built a community*. Magination Press.

Jerome Pohlen (2016). *Gay & lesbian history for kids: The century-long struggle for LGBT rights*. Chicago Review Press.

Rob Sanders (2020). *Mayor Pete: The story of Pete Buttigieg*. Henry Holt and Company.

Rob Sanders. (2018.) *Peaceful fights for equal rights*. Simon & Schuster Books for Young Readers.

Rob Sanders (2018.) *Pride: The story of harvey milk and the rainbow flag*. Random House.

Rob Sanders (2021). *Stitch by stitch: Cleve Jones and the AIDS memorial quilt*. Magination Press.

Rob Sanders (2019). *Stonewall: A building. An uprising. A revolution*. Random House.

Rob Sanders (2021). *Two grooms on a cake: The story of America's first gay wedding*. Little Bee Books.

Thank you to Suzanne Manford Swan and PFLAG for their assistance with this project.

With thanks to my sister, Pat Sanders, whose support and encouragement have never wavered—RS

For my mom—SK

Magination Press

Books for Kids From the
American Psychological Association
maginationpress.org

Magination Press is a registered trademark of the American Psychological Association. Order books at maginationpress.org, or call 1-800-374-2721.

Book design by Rachel Ross
Printed by Phoenix Color, Hagerstown, MD

Cataloging-in-Publication Data is on file at the Library of Congress

Print ISBN: 9781433840203
Print LCCN: 2021062856
Electronic ISBN: 9781433840258
Electronic LCCN: 2021062857

Manufactured in the United States of America
10 9 8 7 6 5 4 3 2 1